STRIVING TO SURVIVE

THE HUMAN MIGRATION STORY

BEN WOOD JOHNSON

TESKO
TESKO PUBLISHING
Pennsylvania

Middletown, Pennsylvania
Tesko Publishing

Copyright © 2020 Tesko Publishing E-book Edition
Copyright © 2020

Ben Wood Johnson

Johnson, Ben Wood
Striving to Survive: The Human Migration Story/Ben Wood
Johnson.—Tesko Publishing ed.

ISBN-13: 978-1-948600-17-0 (Paperback)
ISBN-10: 1-948600-17-X

Johnson, Ben Wood
Striving to Survive: The Human Migration Story

Tesko Publishing website address: www.benwoodjbooks.com

Eduka Solutions
330 W. Main St. #214
Middletown, PA 17057, USA

Printed in the United States of America

To my children and to my children's children

The inevitability of death is not a reason to surrender to it at
any point in your life. —Dad (June 2019)
BWJ/BAW

I would like to thank my God for giving me the strength to carry on in this treacherous world. I would like to thank my eldest son (Wood) for helping me put this book together.

CONTENTS

Preface.. *vii*

Introduction.. *1*

1. The Promise of Survival.................................. 11

2. Extraordinary Men's World 21

3. Under Constant Assault 31

4. Good Living Conditions 41

5. The Human Migration Story............................ 53

6. Navigating a Dangerous World 65

7. Life is an Eternal Struggle 81

v

8. The Art of Survival 93

    Conclusion *103*

    Author's Note *109*

    About the Author *115*

    Other Info *117*

    Index *119*

    Other Works *133*

PREFACE

WHAT IS THE EXTENT of human survival? Is survival always a guarantee? Is it the case that every man shall enjoy freedom, liberty, and the pursuit of happiness? Is there a link between survival and immigration? Why people migrate from one place to another? Is there a safe place for men on earth? Was life meant to be difficult? Would the human kind ever master the art of survival?

I admit that these are complex questions. While there are no right answers, there are no wrong answers either. Nonetheless, the next few chapters will sketch out several probable explanations, which you might find informative or even intellectually intriguing.

This book includes several short essays, which debate the upshots of human survival. Because of the span of the manuscript, the arguments I proposed here only provide an outline of the realities people may face on foreign lands. The hope is to clarify the traits of human endurance.

The theories I will echo throughout this work stemmed from personal situations. As an immigrant, I have been in the trenches. Bear in mind that my approach is mainly philosophical. Still, I promise no objectivity in this work.

Indeed, I have a noteworthy perspective. I left my home many years ago. During that time, I found myself in situations, which made me questioned the purpose of my existence. These moments made me question the degree to which my life is relevant. They made me ponder on my chances of survival in a milieu where living a decent life is nearly impossible.

After more than two decades of wandering in futility on foreign lands, I am a bit cynical about my prospects now. I am perplexed of my likelihood of preserving my beingness. I am no longer certain of being able to consolidate my efforts to guarantee my continued existence on foreign soils, considering that many others are struggling in vain to secure their own in the same milieu.

Over the years, I learned about the roots of my troubles. I uncovered the causes of my situations. I learned about my social milieu. In the process, I learned to accept my reality. I had to find the means to survive against all odds. I had to strive to survive.

This work is a snappy, but to the point, relation of the reality of immigrants. The emphasis is on the struggles a person might face in places where foreigners are not welcome. To reiterate, I have a distinctive view about the immigration story. I hope to share it with you as candidly as possible.

The goal is to assess the ontology of human survival by referring to real-world situations. The text explores some of the hurdles a person might face in his quotidian. It examines the realities that typify a foreign social milieu.

While this work is not comprehensive, it depicts, though summarily in this case, the dynamic between those who already settled on a land and newcomers. The idea is to reflect on the evils a person might face during his search for continued existence away from home.

This collection is relatively short. As you might expect, it does not delve in complicated philosophical notions. It does not examine abstract concepts. But in this opus as well, I encourage those who face tough times on unfamiliar terrains to effort to survive. I encourage them to do so no matter what their state of affairs might be.

If you would like to learn more about the link, I propose between human survival and human migration patterns, I encourage you to read this text cover-to-cover. If you would like to learn about my philosophical writings in general, I encourage you to see my other works. You may find them listed toward the end of the document.

Good Reading!

Ben Wood Johnson, Ph.D.

January 2020

Pennsylvania/USA

Ben Wood Johnson

INTRODUCTION

There is a link between human migration patterns and human survival. That relationship, I will argue in this book, often incites every primal instinct in the being [that is, the human being] to find the means to survive. It may also provide the being the reason (or the reasons) to prevent others from finding the means to do the same.

The being who finds the self under the dominion of another may become combative. He may also become submissive. He may abdicate the self to the whims of the other. Life may become a dangerous adventure.

Survival in an unfamiliar social milieu, I will contend here, can be impossible. The being may have to be creative. He may feel forced to find means to survive by relying on impulses and not on instincts. Many immigrants know this inevitability too well.

In this pamphlet, brief though it is, considering the nature of the viewpoints I will echo in it, I propose to explore the aforementioned link from an idealistic lens. I propose to examine the nature of human survival in a foreign milieu by referencing my own experience in similar environments. I will itemize the adventure of immigrants in places where being foreign could be akin to a death sentence.

I could not speak for all immigrants here. The immigration experience is personal. The ups and down of the journey on foreign lands may vary. The length or the intensity of this trial may depend on a person's internal strength. It may also depend on the person's mental faculty to see the world for what it is and not how others project it to him.

If you happen to be an immigrant, you might have experienced a different reality on foreign lands. Depending on where you evolve, your immigration journey might be different from mine. Your reality might be a wonderful tale. It might be a story worth cherishing with the world. I guess what I am saying here is that my perspective about immigration might differ from your own.

My immigration experience was [perhaps still is] awful. It is far from what I expected. During my journey, I have found solace in knowing that I am not alone.

Over the years as well, I have found out that the immigration story is somewhat similar across the board. Most people did not leave their home just because they felt like it. Many a time, the urge to leave came from a motivation to escape a putrid social reality.

People often immigrated somewhere other than their homeland because of the precocity of their lives in that milieu. Other times, it is because of a necessity to survive against the odds. The enthusiasm to leave the motherland may also be the result of a need to survive beyond chance.

Sometimes, people left their home because they learned about how others are living the good life in certain places. Time and again, people left their homeland in a search of a better life.[1] Often as well, their departure was

---

[1] Most modern societies are described as places of refuge. One place in particular is known as a "Shining City on a Hill." This is a reference to President Ronald Reagan's farewell address to the nation in 1989. Please visit the following link if you would like to learn more. https://www.presidency.ucsb.edu/documents/farewell-address-the-nation

provoked by the promise of survival itself. But that promise, more often than not, turned out to be a fantasy.

Whatever the case may be, the being must carry on wherever he may be. The being must find ways to exist in his new world. He must find the means to subsist by right and not by chance. The problem is that doing so could be next to impossible.

PART I

CHAPTER ONE

THE PROMISE OF SURVIVAL

In the natural, every man is entitled to a long life. Every man must have an equal chance to pursue his [own] happiness. Every man must enjoy freedom. Every man must be *libre* under his skin. Every man is entitled to liberty.

Ideally, every man must survive. Better yet, any man should be able to survive in places where survival itself is likely. But every man should only be able to strive to survive anywhere in the world as long as it is possible to do so. This is what I call *Natural*

11

Equity. We could also refer to this transcendence state within the natural as the *Equity of Survival.*

I would concede that some people might say the preceding claims are only ideals. By themselves, they have no tangible weight in the real world. Therefore, they have no real bearing in the world of men today. These notions are just *palabres* or simple rhetoric.

Although most modern men would swear by these principles, for they learned about them in books, many of them would concede (although privately of course) that these notions are nothing but ideals, which some wise men enshrined on a piece of paper somewhere or at some point throughout the Middle Ages.[1] In consequence, they are not

---

[1] The Middle Ages include a period in the history of Europe. It lasted between c. 1100 (also known as the era of the fall of the Roman Empire) and 1453 (the fall of Constantinople).

binding. Are these men right? Perhaps they are.

For centuries, the world of men is akin to hell. Most men live in dire circumstances while a few live like kings and queens. Nonetheless, the majority of the men who experience hardships seem okay with their reality.

REFUTING PHILOSOPHICAL AGREEMENTS

Perhaps modern men are not in the wrong. Perhaps philosophical notions about human conducts toward one another were not meant to become the norms of any society, let alone in modern societies. Perhaps they are just moral ideals, which are supposed to apply only in certain circumstances. Perhaps these ideas are not there to guide humankind in their journey on earth. Perhaps the notion of virtue in human beings is overrated.

While the previously noted philosophical ideals are well engrained in the psyche of modern men, many are not sure that they have an obligation toward each other. Indeed, most men of today do not think they are bound by philosophical covenants. Many are not sure whether they should uphold such standards to the letter. In fact, the opposite is always true in places dominated by avarice, materialism, consumerism, greed, and the distasteful folly to uphold a false sense of individualism.

Life can be a daunting experience. But it is more so in a milieu driven by the wants of a few over the needs of many. The happening of men in a social milieu could not be more apart from the notion of natural equity, which I previously noted.

In the real world, none of the philosophical principles mentioned earlier seems to matter. The world of men is split between those who are believed worthy (I call them here, extraordinary men) and those who are believed unworthy (I refer to them here as well as ordinary men). To me, it does not come as a surprise that most modern societies are devoid of humanism.

THE WORTHY MAN

In this scenario, the worthy man is special. He holds a certain degree of exceptionalism, which sets him apart from his kind. It is as if he had been placed on earth by a divine being. We could call that divinity "God."

The worthy man holds out of the ordinary traits. His skin oozes purity; he is white like the snow that falls from the sky. He is above his nature. He is angelic; he is righteous.

The worthy man has exceptional talents. He is cultivated; he is cultured; he is sophisticated; he is erudite from head to toe.

The worthy man is close to being perfect. Not only is he a do-gooder, he is virtuous at his core being. Simply put, he is a good man.

The worthy man has no equals. He is a man of science; he is rational; he is well balanced; he is from the heavens. Thus, the worthy man is extraordinary.

THE UNWORTHY MAN

The unworthy man, on the other hand, is the reject of the earth. He comes from the bowels of the planet. He is a scourge. He embodies evil; he is the darkness. His skin oozes malevolence.

The unworthy man is mischievous. He is acidic. He is prone to violence. He could be vicious.

The unworthy man is uncultured. He has no past; he has no present; he has no future.

The unworthy man has no ancestral heritage worthy of acknowledgement. His presumed ancestors are random subjects who once roamed arid lands on the planet. He has no talent. He is a burden on the worthy man.

The unworthy man does not know where he comes from. He does not know where he is. He has little notion of boundaries. He has no idea where he is headed.

The unworthy man is unrefined; he is rancorous. He is under the grip of his nature. He is irrational; he is mundane; he is vain; he is irrelevant.

The unworthy man is greedy. He is easily corrupted. He is lazy; he prefers easy spoils. He deserves nothing but what comes to him. Thus, the unworthy man is always ordinary.

Ben Wood Johnson

CHAPTER 2

Extraordinary Men's World

In the world of extraordinary men, the ordinary man does not deserve life. He has no interest in freedom. He wishes happiness neither for himself nor for others. He is perhaps nature's biggest anomaly. On this earth, he does not belong.

In the world of extraordinary man, living the good life is always expected. But living in poverty is unnatural. It is like a curse.

Every extraordinary man is supposed to live a dignified lifestyle. Of course, that belief generally stems from a sense of entitlement. In the world of extraordinary men as well, the capacity to live the good life is passed down from one generation to the next.

In the world of extraordinary men, certain men shall never experience the hard life. The reason, some are convinced, is that these men come from a long line of extraordinary men, many of whom have accomplished extraordinary things in the history of the humankind.[1] These men's places are well established in the pantheon of great men. They embody greatness.

In the world of extraordinary men, the ordinary man matters less. In such a milieu, no ordinary man is entitled to freedom; no ordinary man is entitled to liberty; no

---

[1] If your parents experienced the good life, you are likely to enjoy the same. This is generally the case regardless of your inherent capacity to survive on your own. The opposite is also true. That is, if your parents were poor, you are likely to experience a lingering state of poverty.

ordinary man is entitled to the pursuit of happiness; no ordinary man is entitled to life, let alone the good life.

PROVING THE SELF WORTHY

In the world of extraordinary men, the ordinary man has to prove himself worthy. But such a demarche is always in hollowness. Against all odds, the ordinary man has to carve himself a place to survive. Against all odds, the ordinary man must carry on. He must do so even when he could not survive on his own.

Against his nature, the ordinary man must accept his reality. He must do so even when he could not bear that actuality. That is the only way for the ordinary man to enjoy any state of mind, which may resemble instances of freedom, life, liberty, and the pursuit of happiness.

In the world of extraordinary men, no matter the extent to which the ordinary man prospered, he will never reach the rank of an extraordinary man. In the world of extraordinary men, the ordinary man will always be ordinary. This is to say that in the world of extraordinary men, the ordinary man will inexorably remain ordinary.

ORDINARY MEN'S WORLD

There is a world of a difference between the ordinary and the extraordinary men. In the world of ordinary men, there is no guarantee of survival. In the world of ordinary men, life has no value beyond that attached by extraordinary men. In the world of ordinary men, survival is a gimmick.

In the world of ordinary men, achieving the good life is a pointless pursuit. The ordinary man seldom experiences something akin to the good life. Those who are lucky enough to experience such a life would never know its full extent.

For the ordinary man, knowing the good life is always ephemeral. His success is short-lived. But his failures are always long lasting.

In the world of ordinary men, the ordinary man must earn the good life. When he succeeds, he must cherish his good fortunes. He must preserve the newly acquired good life at all costs. In the world of ordinary men, good living conditions stem from extraordinary men.

In the world of ordinary men, knowing the hard life is a rite of passage. The ordinary man has no choice but to suffer. In the middle of his calamities, the ordinary man must become extraordinary. But he will never receive this title.

In the world of ordinary men, knowing difficult times is an inescapable crusade. In the world of ordinary men, experiencing vicissitudes is by default. In the world of ordinary men, life can be an unpleasant experience.

No Guarantee of Survival

In the world of ordinary men, there is no guarantee of continued survival. This is so no matter whom the ordinary man thinks of himself. This is so no matter where the ordinary man finds himself. This is so no matter where the ordinary man comes from. This is so no matter where the ordinary man intends to go.

In the world of ordinary men, life can be a daunting experience. In the world of ordinary men, finding the means to survive anywhere on this rock called earth can pose an enormous challenge. In the world of ordinary men, life can be difficult to a point where death might become tempting.

One could make the case that the adventure of ordinary men in the world of extraordinary men today is not that cynical. In the world of men in general, survival has never been promised to any man. This understanding is well established throughout antiquity.

Even among extraordinary men, there is no consensus about which faction should prosper. That is the reason men, be they ordinary or extraordinary, have always been the most lethal enemies of their kind. Men have always despised one another. Men have always undermined the livelihood of one another. Men, be they ordinary or extraordinary, have always been at war with one another.

CHAPTER 3

UNDER CONSTANT ASSAULT

Life itself is a constant struggle. Men are continuously under assault. They are battered relentlessly by the natural elements. They are assaulted unremittingly by one another. It is a constant fight for survival.

Every entity in the natural milieu wants to seize men. Even men want to appropriate themselves. At his intrinsic state, a man's beingness is seen as a commodity, which is worth possessing.

The history of men is that of a continuous struggle against their kind. Men have always endeavored, at times, teeth and nails, to own men. Men tend to consume men as food; men practice cannibalism. For these reasons, men must be unrelenting in their pursuit for continued survival, for death (either from the natural or from other men) is always around the corner.

Within the natural, a man's ambitions are inconsequential. His dreams are incidental. His continued survival is all but certain.

Regardless of the truth of either the ordinary man or the extraordinary man, life is never an experience, which a man should take lightly. But it is not just a man's verity. When it comes to survival in the natural, no particular living entity enjoys any priority.

There is a codependency within the natural milieu itself. In this instance, every existence is intertwined. As a result, one entity often lives off the life of another.

A caution is worth outlining as we move along in this diatribe. Survival in a social milieu could be impracticable. As noted earlier, the struggle in a social milieu is between those who are believed worthy and those who are considered unworthy.

In such a place, there is always a reason for the entity (or the person) whose life is believed unworthy to be on the offensive. There is always a reason for the ordinary man to be on the defensive, for he is always under assault from those who may consider him unworthy. In any case, the being must thrive. He must survive against all odds.

STRIVING TO SURVIVE

The extent of human survival is closely dependent on the milieu where the person evolves. Apart from the idea that some men are convinced that they are better than others are, there is an unpleasant fact, which few men could deny. The natural brings the best out of the human being. But this is not necessarily true for a social milieu.

Society brings the worst out of the being. There, survival is always selective. Being granted the means to survive could be the result of the fancy of someone else.

In a social milieu as well, life could be a scolding experience. People often find it hard to meet their basic needs. In similar locals, finding food could be a challenge. Finding employment could be next to impossible. Finding shelter could be difficult.

Being able to take care of the self could also be a complicated affair. The being may feel the need to abdicate the self to the whim of those who control the milieu. That veracity could easily become a source of inner turmoil in the person.

34

People may feel a sense of obligation to slave themselves. They may have to survive by chance. They may subsist only on a day-to-day basis. Even so, there might be no guarantee of continued survival. That is the reason life could be painful, chiefly when it comes to evolving in unfamiliar terrains.

At times, people do not live at all. They may exist under infrahuman conditions. They may exist simply to subsist. As a result, life may become a calamity.

THE TRAGEDY OF LIFE

Life is not always a crucible. The living experience could be bearable. Still, certain places could be more dangerous for some individuals than they might be for others.

In similar settings, life could become a burden; life could become a curse. Under these circumstances, life could also become a horrible experience. Then, life could become a tragedy for the being.

The selective nature of a social milieu may make life precarious. Surviving in such a milieu could be a depressing experience. Life could become a hindrance rather than a pleasurable experience.

The being may succumb to the weight of his life. He may become disillusioned about his own existence. He may become estrange to the struggles others face in their world. He may become numb to the pain and sorrow caused by being in the milieu. The being may surrender the self to the thrift of the social milieu itself.

While a life is supposed to be lived in its fullest, the conditions or the status quo in which a person finds the self may make life unbearable to a point where the person may dread the living experience altogether. He may even want to end his life prematurely.

This grim reality may increase the fragility of life. It may make life precarious to a point where the bearer of the life itself could become the most lethal threat to that life. The being could engage in self-mutilation. He could engage in self-deprivation. The being could immerse the self in self-deprecation.

CHAPTER 4

GOOD LIVING CONDITIONS

Despite the begrudging nature of life anywhere in the world, it was not designed to be a tragic experience. Despite of everything, good living conditions may be accessible. Without a doubt, living the good life is largely a reward, at least for most.

In certain environments, the good life is a privilege. Many seek it. However, only few could enjoy it. As well, the good life is rarely afforded to a person who is deemed unworthy.

The common understanding in extraordinary men circles is that the ordinary man was not designed to enjoy the good life. He would not know what to do with that life if he were to be given the chance to experience it.

For the ordinary man, living the good life is a goal, which he must always pursue. He is also aware that he shall never attain it. Thus, the pursuit itself often becomes a source of meaning for the ordinary man.

Some might say that the search for meaning in life is inherent in every human being. That is, a man was born to endeavor. He must effort for the self; he must endeavor for others. In doing so, the man finds himself in the world.

I would not refute the anterior view per se. Nonetheless, it is worth noting that the search for the self is not necessarily the same as searching for comfort. Many a time, a man must first find the self before he could find others. Inexorably, he must first find a means to survive before he could find the time to search for the self.

In a modern social milieu, every search for meaning also entails a struggle for survival. For the ordinary man, it is often a fruitless pursuit, for the search for meaning also entails the search for the good life. But it is not because the ordinary man is greedy or seeks comfort. Rather, it is because he is often denied the basics to live a decent life.

LIVING THE GOOD LIFE

The ordinary man must strive not because he is ambitious; rather, it is because he must survive. For the ordinary man, searching for the good life is a necessity. It is an objective, which he could not always achieve. Bear in mind that searching for the good life is only viable in situations where the being lacks the bare minimum to sustain his life.

For the ordinary man, searching for the good life often becomes an everlasting pursuit for both the self and the meaning of life. In the process, the person often loses the essentiality of the self, which was supposed to help him find the self in the midst of the predicaments, which are often engendered by the social milieu itself.

Some might say that the nature of a human struggle is to live a decent life. I would not refute that viewpoint either. But I would still make the case that the living experience was not supposed to be bearable only for some individuals. I would also echo that any human being should be able to survive anywhere life is possible.

Somehow, we have drifted away from our nature; at least, we have made the natural suffocating for many of us. This is the tragedy, which many of us face in our search for a decent life. More often than not, this is the case when we are away from home. Regardless of our status ante, we become ordinary men in a new social space.

Another reason the living experience could be unbearable is worth noting here as well. In this case, it is the restrictive nature of the milieu where we evolve. We may be confined both in our mind and in our body. That materiality often increases the depressing nature of life in a social milieu.

LIVING IN A FANTASY WORLD

The world of men can be an illusion; it can be a mirage in a desert. It can be a deception.

In a social milieu, life may not be what it seems. Life may not be the manner in which it materializes. Life may not be the manner in which it comes into view. The environment itself could be even more toxic than it looks, at least underneath the surface.

For many of us, figuring out the social milieu could be a source of internal turmoil. Most people could not navigate the reality that they face in their quotidian. Some could not do so simply because there are not familiar with the milieu.

A social setting is restrictive by design. Those limits are in the forms of laws and rules, which are not only arbitrary, but are also enforced [customarily, I would say] in the most egregious manners. This *tour de force* often creates a need in the being to strive to remain alive.

Despite the nature of the social milieu one evolves, there is always the chance that one's conditions might change. There is always the chance that one's sordid crusade might ameliorate. There is always hope. But hope is not necessarily a good thing for the being.

Hope could be a curse. It could be a drag. It could become demoniac. It could bring all sorts of evil in the life of the being. It would not be far-fetched to say that hope is the engine of human misery on planet earth. It often induces human beings to endure, even when enduring could be harmful to the person's own welfare.

No Way Out

Life can be a dead end. The being may be stuck. In certain environments, there can be no way out. There can be no reprieve.

Bearing one's life in a social milieu may become an everlasting struggle, in which the being would only know defeat. In the long and dangerous fight to stay alive, the being would never prevail. Yet, the being must persist in that pursuit.

For most, life may become a vapid endeavor, which they could not abandon while being in a conscious state of mind. It is like a gamble, which the being is certain to lose in the end. It is like a bet, which the being could not prevent the self from placing against the self.

The chances of continued survival may depend on the setting where the person finds the self at a particular moment. To reiterate, there is a co-dependency between wanting to survive and being granted the means to do so. The irrefutable amalgamation between a person's want[1] to survive and the reality the individual may face in his journey to finding the means to survive is worth examining further.

---

[1] Even the individual's capacity to survive could make a difference in certain cases.

PART II

CHAPTER 5

THE HUMAN MIGRATION STORY

M igration is the story of humanity. Human beings are nomadic in their core beingness. Because of our tendencies to venture on unfamiliar terrains, we never stayed in one place.

For millennia, human beings have traveled from one location to another. Since we have found ourselves in this world— supposedly, I must say—we have been searching for it everywhere else. We are on a constant search for meaning.

We have gone to places; we have been to places. We are always on the move. We are migrants by nature. But an important truth about human migration patterns is worth considering here as well.

The chronicles of human resettlements are often romanticized to a point of shallowness. The definiteness of the human journey on the planet [earth] entails tales of tragedies and moments of atrocious calamities, which we are likely to overlook. We have a tendency to aggrandize the human experience even though we know that it is, in the main, a tragic and, at times, a fatal experience. We live in denial.

THE HUMAN EXPERIENCE

There are countless stories about the human experience. Some of them are true accounts or they reflect real events. Other stories are mythical recites. In this case, they did not happen for real or they happened only to a certain extent. Still, these stories constitute our understandings of the human journey in their environments.

These stories are likely to depict the truism of the humankind on earth in a *quixotic* manner. Men have a tendency to raise themselves to a status of God. But men's own accounts of themselves are often far from the happening of the humankind.

These legends, if I could refer to them that way, usually outline the plight of the species to belong. They claim to tell us about the human sacrifice to uphold their significance in their world. Many of these stories have a happy ending. But to repeat myself, this is seldom the case in the real world.

The human story is that of tragedy. It seldom ends in allegory. The joy of birth is never comparable to the sorrow of death.

Every human story ends with a series of events, which led to the death of someone dear or someone others unreservedly despised. Either way, there can be no joy in the death of another person. One man's passing is a staunch reminder of another man's fate.

No living being is important to a point where the value of his life supersedes that of another. The same is true for men. No man is omnipotent within the natural. Regardless of a man's social rank or status, he must face death.

It does not matter whether the man is ordinary or extraordinary, he could not defeat death on its own turf. No matter how allegoric the story of a man begun, it is certain to end on a tragic note. No matter how great a man was, just like a *banana leaf* or just like a *palm tree leaf*, he will fold to the ground. Regardless of a man's talents or his accomplishments, he is not (or he could never be) immortal.

The tragic nature of the human existence itself may make you wonder (at times) whether human beings had been designed to be on this planet. We are so fragile in this milieu that our existence is almost inconsequential. We are so irrelevant in the natural that we find meaning only by making ourselves meaningless. One man is grand only when another is not.

Before the trials we face in this place called earth, it is probable that we might be misplaced beings. That is why it often makes sense to ponder on the following questions: Who are we? Why are we here? Where are we headed? What is the meaning of our existence?

I would admit it here; I do not have any answers regarding the preceding questions. It would be presumptuous on my part to suggest otherwise. All the same, it would not be fanciful to say the human existence is like a malediction. Here is why I say that...

Regardless of our eventuality, we are supposed to live on this planet. In this volatile milieu as well, I would reiterate, survival is promised to no one. But what are we to do? Well, we must survive. We must recognize that we are stuck here.

As a living being, uncovering that truth could be depressing. It may make you sad. That discovery may make you question the feasibility (or even the practicability) of your [own] existence.

HUMAN VERACITY

While there are many approaches to explaining the human experience, most accounts, if I may say so, are atypical to the circumstances that a human being might face during a lifetime. Uncovering that veracity may make the human experience depressing. The being may think that he is the only living entity who is experiencing a squalid life.

Another aspect of the human odyssey on earth worth outlining here is the notion of belonging. The understanding in this case is that humans long for companionship. Human beings want to belong, they say.

The truth about the supposed human fondness for companionship is that human beings are the biggest threats to their species. None could take a man's life faster than another man's resentment. None could be more lethal to men than men themselves are.

Belonging, at least for some, is not always possible; it may not be feasible; it may not even be recommended. Sometimes, it is best for some men to stay away from certain men. I would go a bit further here.

I would echo that men were not designed to stay in one place. Human beings were made to wander their environments. This is the essence of human survival. In certain places, I must also admit, human wandering could easily become penitence.

The human definiteness is that people are condemned to wander the planet. They must do so in a search for a suitable place to call home.[1] Meanwhile, they may lose the self. They may lose their sense of direction. That is the nature of the human migration story.

To say it again, the human nature is to wander their world. This is how human beings evolve in their milieu. A person learns about his nature by exploring the surroundings. But that natural keenness, I must also echo, could be harmful. It could

---

[1] Bear in mind that no home is fixed or permanent.

lead the person to dangerous paths in the pursuit for survival.

CHAPTER 6

NAVIGATING A DANGEROUS WORLD

There is no safe place for men on earth. There is no question about that understanding either. Human beings live on a dangerous planet. For this reason, the primary goal of our existence is to avoid danger at all costs.

As a fragile entity on the planet, we must strive [at times, every second of our existence] to stay away from environments, which might be lethal to our beingness. We must avoid realities, which might be dangerous to our kind. We must elude entities, which we might make out as being lethal for our existence. This is the nature of our lived experience on planet earth.

Despite our determination to stir clear from danger, we could not always avoid dangerous conditions in the milieu where we evolve. We have to adapt; we have to adjust. We have to be practical; we have to anticipate. This is the best way for us to survive beyond chance.

An important truth is worth noting at this point. That is, the circumstances of men in the natural milieu often differ from the problems they face in the artificial setting (that is, in society). Men often have to fiddle with their factuality, be it environmental, social, or supernatural, to make sense of it all. In similar places, men must do whatever it takes to stay alive. They must do so whether their circumstances might come from the natural or whether they might come from the artificial.

No matter where we are on the planet, as human beings, we face challenges. Life in and of itself can be a calamity. No God or God-like figures could help us surmount our depressing contingencies, for they are likely caused by men themselves. No matter what our circumstances might be, we must endure.

Nature equips every human being with the tools and the techniques to further his existence in the face of calamities. The problem is that the artificial milieu strips our ability to find the means to strive to survive. We are always vulnerable in such a milieu.

All right, we are likely to persevere anywhere on the planet. We are likely to endure. But the odds are always against us in the social milieu.

While life was meant to be difficult for us on earth, it was not meant to be impossible. But we often lose ourselves in an attempt to preserve the self, many a time, in idleness. We are often lost in our social happening. That truth often aggravates our vulnerability in our world.

Sometimes, we lose ourselves by choice, be it consciously or subconsciously. Other times, it is by design. There are times as well when we might be induced to overlook our own truth to the harm of our own survival needs.

Life, I must resound, is a continuous struggle. In this case, the being, to his unfathomable disillusionment, is condemned to survive in his world even when survival might not be possible or even feasible. Still and all, the being may have no choice but to strive to survive.

There can be no living without striving. There can be no striving without meaning. Omitting as well, finding meaning in this volatile world is not only a personal undertaken but it is also a death-defying venture, which, to reiterate, the being could not escape.

Few people have the stamina to aim for any sense of meaning in life beyond what is obvious to the naked eye. For most, life is an adventure. From their vantage point, "you lose some; you win some." For these people, the living experience is a commodity, which they may trade for anything but life itself. They live in the moment. They often see no need to struggle beyond their made out capacity to do so. But life is not always rosy for them.

When life takes unexpected turns, these people are likely to falter in their search for survival. If not, they may surrender to their factuality. They may seek to escape their reality. They may do so by any means available.

When life becomes unlivable, the person might find it necessary to effort shamelessly, some might say, to preserve their ideal lifestyle. When life becomes unbearable, they may engage in conducts that they might have never considered or even tolerated. They may do drugs; they may do crimes; they may become promiscuous; they may become violent. They may become resentful. They may blame others for their misfortunes.

When the substantiality of life becomes physically untenable or mentally unbearable, these people would likely recoil in a safe space. That space could be the social milieu, which bred the calamity they are facing. That reality often incites the being to become selfish.

The being may see others as impediments to his [own] survival. He may strive relentlessly to undermine the capacity of others to survive. Those who are considered unworthy of being in the social milieu may become scapegoats.

THE FRAGILITY OF LIFE

In a social milieu, life could become more precarious than it is supposed to be. There, the being does not have the tools or the techniques to face his troubles. The being is left to fend for the self. But he is generally left to do so empty-handed.

Life could become unsustainable. It could become an endless descent to hell. It could become an everlasting plight for survival.

The person who is judged unworthy of life is sure to be victimized every step of the way. This happening may create an atmosphere of fear. That climate may be reinforced by the rules and other control methods put in place specifically by the man who believes himself to be worthy to devalue those that he deems unworthy.

The cynicism of the social milieu may make life uncertain for most. The environment may become a jungle where every man (or every group of men) could be left to effort (in vain at times) for the self. That discovery may also induce men to despise both the self and the other.

Subtle differences or nuances in skin tone, differences in culture, disparities in ethnicity, distinctions in religion, or even incompatibilities in ways of life may provide the others the necessary motives to effort, painfully at times, for the permanency of an unfathomable state of social exclusions. These people may worsen discriminatory [if not cruel] practices against those they consider different. These conditions may incite the being to see the other as a threat to his [own] survival.

Under similar regimes, hate may become a norm in the social milieu. The other may be sensed as an impediment or even a menace, which must be tamed or uprooted at all costs. In this case, life may become indefensible. Human existence, in its most intrinsic sense, may become unbearable.

STRIVING TO STAY ALIVE

Life may become unlivable. In the middle of this undeniable fragility, some people may have no alternatives but to strive stubbornly to stay alive. The individual may feel the need to effort, violently at times, to make it on his own by any means necessary. This understanding may encourage the being to behave in a way that may lead to his premature death or that of another.

For others, the essence of the struggles they face in the social milieu is what gives meaning to their journey through life. For them, the obstacles they face often strengthen the living experience itself. No matter what—from their vantage point—life must go on; they must endure. These people consider themselves "survivors."

There are those who are inquisitors. They do not accept life as is (or as it is presented to them). They are in an everlasting search for answers beyond a mere sensory understanding of the world around them. They seek answers beyond what is readily available. These people [like me, if I may say so] are beyond a mere surviving mode.

The inquisitors are likely to survive beyond chance. These people are trying to make sense of the reason they must survive in a world designed purposefully to take away their beingness. Although they want to survive, they would prefer to do so outside the orb of serendipity. Of course, this is not always possible.

The inquisitors, as described here, live in an everlasting state of sorrow. They are miserable to death. They know that life itself is a tragedy. But they could not escape from it.

For the inquisitors, life is always gloomy. They feel powerless. They feel obligated to live through the calamity of life by any means necessary. This is the roots of their pain.

THE CHALLENGES OF SURVIVAL

While great efforts to uncover the natural in its magnificence could be rewarding, the struggle to belong in a new social milieu could be fatalistic. In similar settings, the trials one faces do not increase the value of the living experience itself. Rather, they are likely to poison it. Then again, there is little chance of avoiding that eventuality.

When it comes to finding oneself a place to be in this world, the hurdles one might face could be insurmountable, markedly for the ordinary man. The long road [and sometimes the treacherous journey] toward finding oneself a place to belong in the world of extraordinary men could be laden with obstacles, some of which could lead to premature death. That is why during the hunt for continued existence, there is always a need to be cautious. This verity could not be more vivid for an immigrant, above all for those who live in a hostile social milieu.

Of course, when it comes to finding a means for survival on foreign lands, not every immigrant would fall in the same category. Some people are more resilient than others are. Regardless of the predicaments one might face on an unfamiliar social milieu, the person must deal with his new factuality. He must do so on his own, for his own, and with his own. Granted, doing so might also pose a challenge for the being.

CHAPTER 7

LIFE IS AN ETERNAL STRUGGLE

L ife could be understood as an eternal struggle. But that does not mean that life should be unbearable. That does not mean that life should be a burden for the being.

Yes, the moment you were born, you have to fight to stay alive. You have to be. You have to preserve your beingness. Even so, you must recognize that fighting to stay in the circle of life is a battle, which many of us lose, often prematurely, I might add. It is also a battle, which most of us do not want to fight.

Men evolve under the presumption that they have a say in their destiny. For men, they are in control of themselves. Men are taught to take responsibility for events, which they themselves genuinely have no idea as to why they happened.

Men are also torn between what is and what they presume. On the one hand, men often feel confident about the purpose of their actions. On the other hand, they are not resolute about the nature of their omissions or their commissions.

In spite of men's ambivalence in their world, they are filled with pride. But a man's hubris could also be to his own demise. While men believe they have a say in their own prognostics, they are not certain of the nature of their illness. Even though men presume that they have the final say so in their [own] destiny, they doubt this is the case in the real world. That is why men vacillate between the real and the possible.

Despite our made out will (or regardless of our determination) to be a certain way, we were thrust into this world with the innate want to be the best that we could be. As well, being all that we could be, I must nevertheless insist, is not always feasible. Sometimes, it is not even possible.

There can be no mastery in the art of survival. Life is a continuous struggle. We must strive to survive. This is the essence of human survival itself.

We must forge a way to be in a world, which exists solely to take away our beingness. That is why our made out role in our calamity on planet earth could only be irrelevant or even inconsequential. We are so long as we could be. Thinking that we hold the key to our own happiness is the irrefutable expression of our sense of self, which also underlines our hubris in a world, which we have no clue about why we found ourselves in it and why we must suffer in it.

Regardless of our circumstances, we must be. Since we were born and until we die, we must engage in an everlasting fight for survival. That veracity is irrefutable for both the ordinary and the extraordinary men.

Another certainty is that we must exist beyond chance. We must carry out our existence by exploring every conceivable avenue to preserve it. By any means available to us, we must strive to survive.

LIFE MUST GO ON

No matter what our circumstances might be, we must negotiate the veracity of our lives. We must suffer. Whatever happens—I must point out here as well—life must go on.

Of course, dealing with the predicaments of our social setting, I must restate, is not always realistic. Sometimes, it is not even recommended. More often than not, we falter in our search for survival. Other times, we give up on ourselves. This is the tragedy of being human in a world controlled by the human species only to ease (or to speed up) the destruction of human beings themselves.

In the face of the realities that we find ourselves, we must further our existence. Despite what our social circumstances might be, we must be beyond chance. We must create certainty for our existence outside the scope of a preordained destiny, which we set up for us, many a time, unwittingly.

Anyway, we must strive to take control of our lives, although we must do so with humility. We must do so by knowing our limits in this dangerous milieu. We must know who we are. We must know where we are. We must understand the reason that we are. We must grapple with the reason others are. We must surmount obstacles to survive. We must find means to be. We must also understand that being is not as simple as we might imagine it to be.

In the face of calamities, we must come up with a strategy to make it out a whole. Under any circumstance, we must survive. We must examine our surroundings. We must be despite someone else's will to let us be.

We must employ ruses; we must use techniques, which would allow us to prolong our existence. We must fight in a relentless struggle to survive; we must preserve our physical integrity; we must uphold our sanity. We must strive to survive.

In the face of it all, we must remain vigilant. Despite it all, we must remain prudent. To say it again, life must go on.

A TRAGICOMIC EXPERIENCE

Life is a tragicomic experience. Every living crusade is both tragic and comedic. The tragedy is the reality one faces. The comedy is the way one deals with the tragedy itself.

Sometimes, we could only laugh at our squalid crusade in life. Laughter could be the best therapy, which could help us deal with some of the most ravaging moments in our life. Other times, we may become immerse in a mental frame of dejection. Whatever the case may be, we must recognize that our state of sorrow alone could catapult us toward our premature end.

For a better or worse, every existence depends on each other. Every life depends on another. This is the nature of the natural milieu. Hence, there is an irrefutable dependency in the natural.

In the social milieu as well, there is a codependency between my beingness and yours. Lives are dependent on one another. What I do or what I omit from doing may affect you in the most intimate manner. The same is true for you toward me. Our existence is also co-dependent.

In the natural, some entities may live on only when they can destroy others. Put differently, some lives may go on only when other lives are no longer. That is, some may exist only when others stop existing.

The notion of mutual existence is not just a natural phenomenon. The concept of co-dependency is part of the artificial as well. In certain social settings, for instance, the same reliance can be irrefutable. It can be palpable. In this context, one entity lives off the fancy of another. It is a war. It is *we* versus *them*.

If truth were told, it would be irrefutable that the aforementioned interdependency is the foundation of most modern societies, most notably those that rely on the collective to further the needs or the wants of the individual. In this instance, for one life to carry on, another life must know destruction. Oftentimes, for one life to carry on, countless other lives must experience some form of destruction.

The being must understand his feebleness in the social terrain where he evolves. He must grasp the nature of the milieu. This may be the only way for him to survive by right and not by chance.

The being must understand that upholding his existence may depend on the extinction of that of another. The being must realize that the "other" might be so powerful that he would stand no chance of withstanding his assaults. The being must realize his limits. He must understand the prospects of his survival chances. The being must come to terms with the possibility that preserving his existence in a place, which had been designed to do away with it, might not be easy.

The being must realize that carrying the self in the world of others might not be possible; it might not be even feasible. The being must recognize that life in a social milieu is not a given. The being must fight for his life. The being must endeavor to maintain his life. The being must also realize that he might perish unnecessarily while upholding his *Beingness* at the wrong time, in the wrong place, and for the wrong purpose.

CHAPTER 8

THE ART OF SURVIVAL

Survival is an art. In spite of everything, there are no experts in the art of endurance. Therefore, there can be no expert in the art of human survival.

Continued existence is not for every living being. What works for one person might lead to the premature death of another. Some will perish; some will thrive. Some will struggle to avoid premature death; others will strive to thrive. In the end, life will go on.

Regardless of the effects of our existence on the materiality others may experience, we must survive. Despite the weight of the existence of others on our own, we must thrive to survive. We must be all that we could be. We must do so at all time and by any means necessary.

No matter what we might be facing, we must uphold our constitution, be it physical, spiritual, psychological, or social. We must be sane. Under any circumstances, we must be. We must find the means to survive beyond serendipity. We must live on to see another day, even if it might be our last.

Of course, the thrift of life often makes it depressing. Once in a while, the conditions of our existence (or the predicaments which we experience) may make striving to stay alive a burden rather than a purpose. For some, finding death by any means necessary may seem like a better alternative to a life of misery.

For those who carry the load of their world on their shoulders [day in and day out], death might seem tempting. Many of us are likely to crumble to the weight of life. Others are weak to the charms of death. Under those circumstances, death might seem like a good escape route from an existence filled with pain and sorrow.

I could not judge those who see their world from such a prism. In saying that, you must also be mindful that a self-inflicted destruction or a self-induced downfall is never the answer to your troubles. You should never harm the self to save the self. Likewise, you should never inflict harm to others as a strategy to save the self.

Sometimes, the self is not worth saving. Sometimes, the best way to survive beyond chance is to stop striving to be altogether.

Sometimes, relinquishing your beingness to the whims of time may be your best, if not your only, option. Sometimes, it may be best to be only to the extent that you could be.

In echoing the previous assertion, I recognize that, for some people, staying alive in a treacherous world might be futile. Some people might think that striving to stay whole is not worthwhile. They might say that it does not make sense to fight *to be* only *to die* in the end. I could understand that.

A NEED TO SURVIVE

Fair enough, I would admit that fighting the natural might not make sense. It is akin to trying to achieve the impossible. Striving to stay alive under harsh circumstances might not even be ideal.

Striving to stay alive in a world of easy death could be a curse. As the members of a vibrant species, we have been on this earth long enough to recognize that our resistance to the predators of our existence could be futile. We know that one way or another, we are going to surrender to their want.

Whatever our situation might be, we must recognize that we are not omnipotent in our world. We must humble ourselves to the truth of our surroundings. We must understand that every living entity on the planet wants to seize our *Beingness* to further their own. But what could we do with that knowledge? I am not sure what to tell you.

Let me ask you this: Do you think that it is of the essence to preserve your *Beingness*? Is it supreme to stay alive in the face of insurmountable troubles? Is it always worth it to fight to stay alive? I would say yes.

Apart from that viewpoint, a few other questions are worth posing as we wrap up this discourse. Why would it be necessary to stay alive? Why your life matters? Could we say that every life matters? Should we say that only certain lives matter or should matter? Should we even say that every life matters or should matter?

Few could answer these fundamental questions objectively. The same is true for me. For this reason, any answer offered here could only be a subjective assessment of the happening human beings are likely to face in their world. I would echo this much, though. Life is a gift. As such, it must be treasured anytime, anywhere, and at all costs.

While the preceding viewpoints may sound trivial to some people, it has an unmistakable intellectual merit, which a living being should never undermine. True, few of us understand the need to preserve the gift of life at all costs. Fewer of us are aware of the predators of our existence. But that lack of awareness, I must nevertheless

point out, could also be a fatal blunder.
Anyway, there is always a need to survive.

WAITING FOR THE AFTER-LIFE

Some people live their present as if it had no
relevance. They live their lives based on the
belief that another life awaits them on the
other side. From their vantage point, this life
does not matter much. Rather, the present
living experience is a test; it is a trial, which
will determine whether they deserve a
chance to live an eternal life on the side of
their savior somewhere in the universe.

The previous understanding, though it
reflects popular religious worldviews, is an
unequivocal miscalculation about the world
of men. In my view, this is an absurdist way
of looking at one's world. Considering the
doubt that surrounds the prospect of existing
[somewhere in the cosmos] after death, I
would not recommend anyone to overlook

the veracity of life in the present moment. There is no guarantee that one would experience life after death in any way, shape, or form.

What I am saying here is that there is no assurance that life would go on after a physical bereavement. There is no certainty of existence after death, at least not at a conscious level. The notion of life after death is perhaps humanity's biggest blind spot. It embodies our wish to be immortal as if the life of an individual was meant to be eternal. Perhaps it is a way for us to preserve our relevance in a world of irrelevance. Perhaps it is our view of our relevance (or the lack of that) in a world of insignificance even after our eventual death.

To be clear, I do not seek to ridicule those who look at their world from such a prism. I must echo as well that I am not sure that another life awaits human beings after death.

If we were realistic, I would say, it would be obvious that there is one life to live. That life is happening right now. Consequently, we should never ignore our existence in the present.

There is always a need to survive once a person is alive. But the need to survive itself may not depend on the individual's want to do so. The need to survive is intrinsic in every being. Such need is a part of our beingness. The struggle to stay alive is what makes the living experience worthwhile.

An important veracity about human survival is also worthy of note here. In this case, regardless of individual approaches to life, we must be alive; we must stay alive. In making this case, I must also admit that staying alive, at least beyond chance, is not always possible.

It is not up to us, as living beings, to stay alive. But it is without doubt within our

reach to strive, perhaps relentlessly, to do so.
We must always strive to stay alive.

CONCLUSION

The ideas I echoed in this manuscript up to this point reflect my own philosophy. They reflect my own journey on foreign lands. I am an ordinary man. I am also an inquisitor.

For more than two decades, I have lived away from the motherland. Coincidentally, survival has always been a big challenge for me. Still, I have preserved my existence in the face of my calamities. I have strived to survive even when I did not think I could do so.

Indeed, I have been an immigrant for a long time now. I have known more days away from my homeland than I foresaw when I left home. In my current state of despondence, I nourish no hope of returning to my birthplace with my head high. I make myself no illusion about the prospects of finding my way back home anytime soon. Yet, I cannot survive outside providence away from the homeland. This is my heartbreak in this world. This is my misfortune.

I must admit it here as well; I am stuck on foreign lands. I do not belong in such places. Sadly, I must nevertheless reckon, it is to my own demise. This is my sordid journey on foreign lands. This is my calamity away from the homeland. I am dying here, however, slowly it might be.

Oh, it has been difficult for me. It has been a horrendous journey. I never expected such a life. I never saw myself that way.

On foreign soils, I have lived some of the worst moments of my life. Despite my gloomy circumstances on distant lands, I long for the day when I would be able to return to my natural roots. I long for the day when I would be able to see my beloved *paysage*. I long for the day when I would be able to be me again. I long for the day when I would be able to head back home, even if I might find myself in a jar, in a coffin, or in a box, for the journey toward my final resting place. This is the reason I strive to survive.

To reiterate, I recognize that in my current social milieu, I am an ordinary man. But I do not envy those who have traced my destiny. I do not resent those who consider themselves extraordinary men.

Not the least, my existence is penitence. I would like to escape it. But my inquisitive nature would not allow me to do so.

I could not surrender myself to the fancy of the other. Nonetheless, I could not be a part of my own death. I have no choice but to strive to thrive. I have no choice but to survive.

On foreign lands, it has not been easy for me. On these exogenous huts, I have become a target; I have been assaulted.

In this despicable social milieu as well, I have dodged death; I have eluded imprisonment. Still I survive; still I strive to live to see another day. Still I go on. I hope you do the same.

While I learned a lot from my ordeal, I understand that my experience is not unique. Most people have gone through terrible times away from their home. Some have perished as a result. Others have made it out okay. But they carry permanent scars in their soul. I am one of them.

No matter what, I must reiterate here, life must go on. No matter how heavy the weight of life might seem, you must endure. You must live to see another day, even if it might be your last. You must strive to survive. You must do so no matter what.

AUTHOR'S NOTE

I LEFT MY HOME several years ago.[1] Since then, I have had to adjust; I have had to adapt. Granted, it has been a terrible journey.

Over the last five years, my life has been at a crossroad. For one reason or another, my world collapsed right under my feet. In a blink of an eye, everything turned upside

---

[1] I left my home in 1997. I immigrated to America soon thereafter. I visited the motherland on a few occasions. But the landscape itself changed for the worst. The people I once knew are gone. I am a stranger in my own country. My heart is filled with sadness. I missed my home.

down. I found myself deprived of means of survival.

Amid my reality, my livelihood became unbearable. I found it difficult to carry on. Still, I thrive. Still, I survive.

My immigration journey left a lasting mark in my soul. I feel battered both on the inside and on the outside my being. I feel lost.

Somehow, I found the wit to resist. I have been able to strive to survive. I have been able to uphold my being at all costs.

I know that I am not alone in this crucible. I am sure that many of you feel down right now. This is not a good time to be an immigrant, especially in countries like the United States, France, and the United Kingdom.

For many of us, it may seem as though the world is broken. It may feel as though someone has banished all the goods and left all the bad peoples in change of the world. It may feel as though all the righteous souls have left the planet.

The despair we feel in our heart could be insurmountable. We may feel rejected. We may feel depreciated.

Indeed, there is a sordid truth about immigration these days. Most immigrant families are experiencing it in a vivid manner. For many, that reality makes no sense. Yet, they are in the middle of it; they have to deal with it.

On foreign lands, immigrants must fend for themselves with their bare fingernails. On foreign lands, immigrants must fight alone against the evils of the world. But they stand no chance of winning this war, which they did not anticipate.

On foreign lands, immigrants are against themselves. They fight a faceless enemy. They face a gutless enemy, who does not fight fair. The enemy knows them extremely well. Although they are not necessarily outnumbered, they are always outsmarted. But on foreign lands as well, the immigrant must survive.

I would also admit that surmounting the obstacles placed before us may seem impossible. Thriving to survive may seem unreal. As a result, life can become burdensome.

Under similar circumstances, we might be prone to quit it all. But many of us are strong. Many of us would never give up. Many of us would never surrender to our continuous state of despair.

On foreign lands, most immigrants are resilient. On foreign lands, most immigrants are relentless. On foreign lands, most immigrants are survivors. On foreign lands as well, most immigrants are inquisitors. No matter what, we will thrive; we will survive.

I would further confess that some of us are not that strong. Some of us are not certain whether we should preserve our beingness. We vacillate in our continuous state of sorrow; we keep on wondering. We go from one place to another. We are in a continuous quest for a better life.

Others may falter before the barrage of assaults brought on by those who thought of themselves as extraordinary men. They may surrender themselves to the whims of the social milieu. They may escape their reality. But I refuse to be that way.

I refuse to live my life as if I did not want it in the first place. I want to survive; I want to live a full life.

On foreign lands, most immigrants are ordinary men. Most of us come from ordinary backgrounds. But we left our home in the search of a better life.

When we immigrate on foreign lands, we are not necessarily striving to become extraordinary men. All we want is the opportunity to live a simple life. All we want is to remain ordinary.

There is no doubt that we are common peoples. But there is no shame in that. Life was perhaps meant to be ordinary. Thus, we are a reflection of life itself.

Although this work was not a recite of my [own] immigration story by itself, I hope the views echoed in it breathed some optimism, however small it might be, in your life. If you would like to learn more, I recommend another text, which is more comprehensive about the subject. See the book titled *"The Anteaters: How to Preserve Your Beingness in a Foreign Milieu* to learn more about my philosophy about immigration.[2]

---

[2] Immigration Philosophy

ABOUT THE AUTHOR

BEN WOOD JOHNSON, Ph.D.

Dr. Johnson is a social observer. He is a multidisciplinary scholar. He writes about Philosophy, Legal Theory, Public and Foreign Policy, Education, Politics, Ethics, Race, and Crime.

Dr. Johnson graduated from Penn State University and Villanova University. He holds a Doctorate in Educational Leadership, a Master's degree in Political Science, a Master's degree in Public Administration, and a Bachelor's degree in Criminal Justice.

Dr. Johnson worked in law enforcement. He attended John Jay College of Criminal Justice. Dr. Johnson is fluent in many languages, including, but not limited to, French, Spanish, Portuguese, and Italian.

Dr. Johnson enjoys reading, poetry, painting, and music. You may contact Dr. Ben Wood Johnson by e-mail or via the postal services.

OTHER INFO

If you would like to contact Dr. Ben wood
Johnson, you may do so by referring to the
information listed below.

ADDRESS
Mailing or Postal Info:

330 W. Main St #214

Middletown, PA

Zip: 17057

EMAIL
E-mail Address: benwoodpost@gmail.com

OTHER INFO

Find Ben Wood on the following media platforms.

Twitter: @benwoodpost

Facebook: @benwoodpost

Blog: www.benwoodpost.com

Website: www.benwoodjohnson.com

Book Store: www.benwoodjbooks.com

Index

A

Abandon, 47
  Abdicate the self, 2, 34
Absurdist way, 99
Actuality, 23
Adventure, 2, 27, 69
Aggrandize, 54
Allegory, 55
  Allegoric, 56
Amalgamation, 48
Ambitions, 32
Ambitious, 43
Ambivalence, 82
Ameliorate, 46
America, 109, 122
Ancestors, 17

Arbitrary, 46
Art, 83, 93, 95, 97, 99, 101
  Art of human survival, 93
  Art of survival, 83, 93, 95,
    97, 99, 101
Artificial (see: Society)
Assault, 31, 33, 35, 37, 89,
  113
  Assaulted, 31, 106
Atmosphere, 71
Atypical, 58
Avarice, 14
Awareness, 98
  Aware, 42, 98
Awful, 3

119

B

Banana leaf, 56
Barrage of assaults, 113
Battle, 81–82
Bearable, 35, 44
Begrudging, 41
Being, 1–2, 5, 13, 15–16,
    33–34, 36–37, 42, 44,
    46–48, 53, 56–60, 65–71,
    73, 77, 81, 83, 85–86,
    89–90, 93, 98, 100–101,
    110
  Beingness, 31, 53, 65, 74,
    81, 83, 87, 90, 96–97,
    101, 113–14
Belief, 21, 99
Bereavement, 100
Beyond, 4, 24, 66, 69, 74,
    84–85, 94–95, 101
  Beyond chance, 4, 66, 74,
    84–85, 101
  Beyond serendipity, 94
Boundaries, 17

C

Calamity, 25, 35, 54, 67,
    70, 75, 83, 86, 103–4

Chance, 4–5, 11, 35, 42, 46,
    48, 66, 74, 76, 84–85, 89,
    95, 99, 101, 111
  Serendipity, 75, 94
Charms of death, 95
Choice, 25, 68, 106
Circumstance, 13, 35, 58,
    66–67, 84–86, 94–96,
    105, 112
Co-dependency, 32, 48,
    87–88
  Dependency, 87
    Dependent, 33, 88
Co-dependent, 88
Combative, 1
Comedy, 87
  Comedic, 87
Comfort, 42–43
Commissions, 82
Companionship, 59
Conscious, 48, 100
  Conscious level, 100
  Conscious state of mind,
    48
  *Continuous state of
    despair,* 112
  Continuous struggle, 32,
    68, 83
Constant, 31, 33, 35, 37, 53

Constant assault, 31, 33, 35, 37
Constant search, 53
Constant struggle, 31
Constitution, 94
  Physical, 86, 94, 100
  Psychological, 94
  Spiritual, 94
Consumerism, 14
Continued, 26, 32, 35, 48, 76, 93
  Continued existence, 76, 93
  Continued survival, 26, 32, 35, 48
Continuous, 32, 68, 83, 112–13
  Continuous quest, 113
Crucible, 35, 110
Cruel, 72
Crusade, 25, 46, 87
Culture, 72
Cynical, 27
  Cynicism, 72

D

Danger, 65–66

Dangerous, 2, 35, 47, 61, 65–67, 69, 71, 73, 75, 77, 85
  Dangerous adventure, 2
  Dangerous conditions, 66
  Dangerous milieu, 85
  Dangerous paths, 61
  Dangerous planet, 65
  Dangerous world, 65, 67, 69, 71, 73, 75, 77
Daunting, 14, 26
Death, 2, 26, 32, 55–56, 73, 75–76, 93–96, 99–100, 106
  Birth, 55
    Birthplace, 104
    Born, 42, 81, 84
  Demise, 82, 104
Defeat, 47, 56
Defensive, 33
Definiteness, 54, 60
Dejection, 87
Depressing, 36, 45, 58–59, 67, 94
  Depressing contingencies, 67
  Depressing experience, 36
  Depressing nature, 45

Despair, 111–12
Despicable social milieu, 106
Despise, 27, 56, 72
Despondence, 104
Destiny, 82–83, 85, 105
  Preordained, 85
Destruction, 85, 89, 95
  Destroy others, 88
Determination, 66, 83
Devalue, 72
Diatribe, 33
Divine (see: God)
  Divinity, 15
Dominion, 1
Drugs, 70

E

Earth, 13, 15–16, 21, 26, 47, 54–55, 57, 59, 66, 68, 83, 96
Effort, 42, 70, 72–73, 75
Egregious, 46
Employ ruses, 86
Endeavor, 32, 42, 47, 90
Endless, 71
Endurance, 93
Enemies, 27
Enforcement, 116

Enjoy, 11, 22–23, 32, 41–42, 116
Entitlement, 22
  Entitled, 11, 22–23
Entity, 31–33, 59, 65–66, 88, 97
Ephemeral, 25
Equity, 12, 14
Erudite, 15
Escape, 4, 69–70, 75, 95, 106, 113
Essence, 60, 74, 83, 97
Estrange, 36
Eternal, 81, 83, 85, 87, 89, 99–100
  Eternal life, 99
  Eternal struggle, 81, 83, 85, 87, 89
Ethics, 115, 121
Ethnicity, 72
Europe, 12
Everlasting, 44, 47, 71, 74–75, 84
Evil, 16, 47, 111
Exclusions, 72
Exist, 5, 35, 83–84, 88
  Existence, 33, 36, 57–58, 65–67, 73, 76, 84–89, 93–95, 97–98, 100–101, 103, 106

Existing, 88, 99

Experience, 2–3, 13–14, 22, 24–26, 32, 34–36, 41–42, 44–45, 54, 58–59, 66, 69, 74–75, 87, 89, 94, 99–101, 106

Extinction, 89

Extraordinary, 15–16, 21–25, 27, 32, 42, 56, 76, 84, 105, 113–14

Angelic, 15

Exceptional, 15

Exceptionalism, 15

Extraordinary man, 21, 24, 32

Extraordinary men, 15, 21–25, 27, 42, 76, 84, 105, 113–14

Cultivated, 15

Cultured, 15

Heavens, 16

Sophisticated, 15

Worthy, 15–17, 23, 33, 72, 101

F

Factuality, 66, 70, 77

Failures, 25

Fair, 96, 112

Families, 111

Fancy, 34, 88, 106

Fantasy, 5, 45

Fatal, 54, 99

Fatalistic, 75

Fate, 56

Fear, 71

Feebleness, 89

Feel, 2, 34–35, 73, 75, 82, 110–11

Feel battered, 110

Feel depreciated, 111

Feel down, 110

Feel rejected, 111

Final, 82, 105

Find, 1–2, 5, 26, 34, 36, 42–44, 48, 57, 67, 70, 85–86, 94, 105, 118, 123

Finding, 1, 26, 34, 48, 69, 76, 94, 104

Find meaning, 57

Find means to survive, 2

Find myself, 105

Find ourselves, 85

Find ways to exist, 5

Foreign, 2–3, 76, 103–6, 111–15

Foreign lands, 3, 76, 103–4, 106, 111–14

Foreign milieu, 2, 114

Foreign policy, 115
Foreign soils, 105
Fragile, 57, 65
   Fragility, 37, 71, 73
Futile, 96–97

G
Gloomy, 75, 105
   Gloomy circumstances,
      105
God, 15, 55, 67
   After-life, 99
      Cosmos, 99
   God-like, 67
Good, 4, 16, 21–25, 41–47,
   95, 110
Great, 22, 56, 75
   Great men, 22
   Greatness, 22
Grim, 37
Gutless enemy, 111

H
Happening, 14, 55, 68, 71,
   98, 101
Happiness, 11, 21, 23, 83
Harm, 68, 95
   Harmful, 47, 60
Harsh circumstances, 96

Heartbreak, 104
Home, 4, 45, 60, 104–6,
   109, 113
   Homeland, 4, 104
Hope, 46–47, 104, 106, 114
   Drag, 47
Horrible experience, 36
Hostile social milieu, 76
Human, 1–2, 13, 33–34,
   42, 44, 47, 53–61, 65, 67,
   73, 83, 85, 93, 98, 100–
   101
   Human being, 1, 13, 34,
      42, 44, 47, 53, 57–60,
      65, 67, 85, 98, 100
   Nomadic, 53
   Human definiteness, 60
   Human existence, 57–58,
      73
   Human experience, 54, 58–
      59
   Human fondness, 59
   Humanity, 53, 100
      Humanism, 15
   Human journey, 54–55
   Humankind, 13, 22, 55
   Human migration, 1, 53–
      55, 57, 59–61
   Human misery, 47
   Human nature, 60

Human odyssey, 59
Human resettlements, 54
Human sacrifice, 55
Human species, 85
Human story, 55–56
Human struggle, 44
Human survival, 1–2, 33, 60, 83, 93, 101
Species, 55, 59, 85, 96
Humble, 97
Humility, 85
Hunt for continued existence, 76
Hurdles, 76

I

Idea, 13, 17, 33, 82, 103
Ideal, 12–14, 70, 96
Overrated, 13
Idealistic lens, 2
Illusion, 45, 104
Immigrate, 4, 109, 114
Immigrant, 2–3, 76, 104, 110–13
Horrendous journey, 105
Infrahuman conditions, 35
Immigration, 2–3, 110–11, 114

Imprisonment, 106
Incite, 1, 70, 73
Inconsequential, 32, 57, 83
Individual, 35, 44, 48, 73, 89, 100–101
Collective, 88
Immortal, 57, 100
Individualism, 14
Inescapable crusade, 25
Inevitability, 2
Inherent capacity, 22
Intrinsic, 31, 73, 101
Innate want, 83
Inner turmoil, 34
Inquisitive nature, 106
Inquisitor, 74–75, 103, 112
Insignificance, 100
Instinct, 1–2
Integrity, 86

J

Journey, 2–3, 13, 48, 54–55, 74, 76, 103–5, 109–10
Joy, 55–56
Judge, 71, 95
Jungle, 72

K

Keenness, 60
Kind, 15, 27, 32, 66
Knowing, 3, 25, 85

L

Landscape, 109
Laugh, 87
  Laughter, 87
Legends, 55
Lethal, 27, 37, 59, 65–66
  Lethal enemies, 27
  Lethal threat, 37
  Lethal to men, 59
  Lethal to our beingness,
    65
Liberty, 11, 22–23
  Libre, 11
    Freedom, 11, 21–23
Life, 2, 4, 11, 14, 21–26,
    32–37, 41–45, 47, 56, 59,
    67–75, 81, 83–90, 93–95,
    97–101, 105, 107, 109,
    112–14, 121
  Burden, 17, 35, 81, 94
    Burdensome, 112
  Gift, 98
  Lifestyle, 21, 70
  Lifetime, 58

Materializes, 45
  Unbearable, 36, 45, 70,
    73, 81, 110
Limits, 46, 85, 89
Livelihood, 27, 110
Lose, 48, 60, 68–69, 81
Lucky, 24

M

Man, 11, 15–17, 21–27, 31–
    33, 42–44, 56–57, 59, 72,
    76, 82, 103, 105
  Men, 12–15, 21–27, 31–
    34, 42, 45, 55–56, 59–
    60, 65–67, 72, 76, 82–
    84, 99, 105, 113–14
    Cannibalism, 32
    Hubris, 82, 84
  Misplaced beings, 57
Materiality, 45, 94
Meaning, 42–44, 53, 57,
    69, 74
Meaningless, 57
Menace, 73
Mental, 3, 87
  Mentally, 70
Middle ages, 12
  Antiquity, 27

Philosophy, 103, 114–15

  Philosophical, 13–14

    Philosophical covenants, 14

    Philosophical ideals, 14

    Philosophical notions, 13

Migration, 53–55, 57, 59–61

  Chronicles, 54

  Migrants, 54

  Migration patterns, 54

  Migration story, 53, 55, 57, 59–61

Miscalculation, 99

Mischievous, 16

Misery, 47, 95

  Miserable, 75

Misfortune, 70, 104

Moral, 13, 121

Motherland, 4, 103, 109

N

Nature, 2, 15, 17, 21, 23, 36, 41, 44–46, 54, 57, 60, 66–67, 82, 87, 89, 106, 122

  Natural, 11–12, 14, 31–32, 34, 44, 56–57, 60, 66–67, 75, 87–88, 96, 105, 121

    Natural milieu, 31–32, 66

Norm, 13, 73

O

Objectively, 98

Obligation, 14, 35, 122

Obstacles, 74, 76, 86, 112

Odyssey, 59

OFFENSIVE, 33

Omit, 88

  Omitting, 69

Omnipotent, 56, 97

Optimism, 114

Ordinary, 15, 17, 22–27, 32–33, 42–45, 56, 76, 84, 103, 105, 113–14

  Anomaly, 21

    Biggest, 21, 59, 100

      Biggest blind spot, 100

      Biggest threats, 59

    Atrocious calamities, 54

    Darkness, 16

    Downfall, 95

Fortunes, 25
Irrational, 17
Mundane, 17
Ordinary man, 22–26, 32–33, 42–44, 76, 103, 105
  Violent, 70
Ordinary men, 15, 24–27, 45, 113
  Accomplishments, 57
  Acidic, 16
  Violence, 16
Ordinary traits, 15
Rancorous, 17
Scourge, 16
Overlook, 54, 68, 99

P

Pain, 36, 75, 95
Painful, 35
Painfully, 72
Palabres, 12
Palm, 56
Palpable, 88
Paysage, 105
Penitence, 60, 106
Physically, 70

Planet, 16–17, 47, 54, 57–58, 60, 65–67, 83, 97, 111
Platforms, 118
Pleasurable, 36
Plight, 55, 71
Precarious, 36–37, 71
Predators, 97–98
Predicaments, 44, 76, 85, 94
Premature, 73, 76, 87, 93
  Prematurely, 36, 81
Preserve, 25, 68, 70, 81, 84, 86, 97–98, 100, 103, 113–14
Preserving his existence, 89
Prognostics, 82
Promiscuous, 70
Purity, 15
Pursue, 11, 42
Pursuit, 23–24, 32, 42–44, 47, 61
  Pursuit of happiness, 23
Putrid social reality, 4

Q
Quit, 112
Quixotic, 55

Quotidian, 46

R

Real, 12, 14, 54–55, 83
  Realistic, 85, 101
  Reality, 3–4, 13, 23, 37,
      46, 48, 65, 70, 85, 87,
      110–11, 113
    Squalid, 59, 87
Recognize, 58, 81, 87, 90,
    96–97, 105
Recoil, 70
Relentless, 86, 112
  Relentlessly, 31, 71, 102
Religion, 72
Resent, 105
  Resentful, 70
Resentment, 59
Resettlements, 54
Reward, 41
  Rewarding, 75
Rhetoric, 12
Righteous, 15, 111
Romanticized, 54
Roots, 75, 105
Rosy, 69
Ruses, 86

S

Sacrifice, 55
Sadness, 109
Safe, 65, 70
Sanity, 86
Savior, 99
Scapegoats, 71
Scars, 107
Scenario, 15
Self, 1–2, 23, 34, 36–37, 42–
    44, 48, 60, 68, 71–72, 84,
    90, 95
  Self-deprecation, 37
  Self-deprivation, 37
  Self-induced, 95
  Self-inflicted, 95
  Self-mutilation, 37
Selfish, 70
Shallowness, 54
Shamelessly, 70
Shelter, 34
Skin, 11, 15–16, 72
Slave, 35
Society, 4, 13, 15, 34, 66–
    67, 88
  Challenge, 26, 34, 67, 75,
      77, 103
  Materialism, 14

Social, 2, 4, 14, 33–34, 36, 43–47, 56, 66–68, 70–77, 85, 87–90, 94, 105–6, 113, 115
  Dominated, 14
  Social circumstances, 85
  Social exclusions, 72
  Social happening, 68
  Social milieu, 2, 14, 33–34, 36, 43–47, 67, 70–77, 87, 90, 105–6, 113
  Social rank, 56
  Social reality, 4
  Social setting, 46, 85, 88
Sordid, 46, 104, 111
Sorrow, 36, 55, 75, 87, 95, 113
Soul, 107, 110–11
Status, 36, 45, 55–56
  Status ante, 45
  Status of god, 55
  Status quo, 36
Story, 3, 53–57, 59–61, 114
  Mythical, 54
Strategy, 86, 95
Strength, 3
  Strengthen, 74

Strive, 11, 43, 46, 65, 67–68, 71, 73, 83–86, 93, 102–3, 105–7, 110
  Striving, 33, 69, 73, 94–96, 114
    Striving to become, 114
    Striving to stay alive, 73, 96
    Striving to stay whole, 96
    Striving to survive, 33
    Striving without meaning, 69
Struggle, 31–33, 36, 43–44, 47, 68–69, 74–75, 81, 83, 85–87, 89, 93, 101
Stubbornly, 73
Subconsciously, 68
Subjective, 98
Submissive, 1
Subsist, 5, 35
Supernatural, 66
Supersedes, 56
Survive, 1–2, 4, 11, 22–23, 26, 33–35, 43–44, 48, 58, 66–68, 71, 74–75, 83–84, 86, 89, 94–96, 99, 101, 103–7, 110, 112–13
  Impulses, 2
  Stamina, 69

Survival, 1–2, 5, 11–13, 15, 17, 24, 26–27, 31–35, 43, 48, 58, 60–61, 68–69, 71, 73, 75–76, 83–85, 89, 93, 95, 97, 99, 101, 103, 110
  Expert, 93
  Gimmick, 24
Surviving, 36, 74
Survivors, 74, 112
Thrive, 33, 93–94, 106, 110, 112

T
Tamed, 73
Tendency, 53–55
Terrains, 35, 53
Therapy, 87
Threat, 37, 59, 73, 122
Thrift, 36, 94
Thriving, 112
Thrust, 83
Trade, 69
Tragic, 41, 54, 56–57, 87
  Tragedy, 35–36, 45, 54–55, 75, 85, 87
  Tragicomic, 87
Traits, 15
Transcendence, 12

Treacherous, 76, 96
  Treacherous journey, 76
  Treacherous world, 96
Trial, 3, 57, 75, 99
Troubles, 71, 95, 97
True, 14, 22, 34, 54, 56, 88, 98
Truism, 55
Truth, 32, 54, 58–59, 66, 68, 88, 97, 111
Turf, 56
Turmoil, 34, 46

U
Undermine, 27, 71, 98
Unfamiliar, 2, 35, 53, 77
Unfathomable, 68, 72
Unique, 106
Unpleasant, 26, 34
Unrelenting, 32
Unwittingly, 85
Unworthy, 15–17, 33, 41, 71–72
Uphold, 14, 55, 86, 89–90, 94, 110

V
Vacillate, 83, 113
Vain, 17, 72

Value, 24, 56, 75
Veracity, 34, 58, 84, 100–101
Verity, 32, 76
Vibrant, 96
Victimized, 71
Vigilant, 86
Virtue, 13
Volatile, 58, 69
Vulnerable, 67
  Vulnerability, 68

W

Wander, 60
  Wander their world, 60
  Wander the planet, 60
Wants, 14, 31, 89, 97
War, 27, 88, 111
Weak, 95
Welfare, 47
Whim, 2, 34, 96, 113
Worth, 3, 31, 33, 42, 45, 48, 54, 59, 66, 95, 97

Y

Your beingness, 81, 96–97, 114
  Your life matters, 97

Your parents experienced, 22

OTHER WORKS

Other works by Dr. Ben Wood Johnson

1. Racism: What is it?

2. Sartrean Ethics: A Defense of Jean-Paul Sartre as a Moral Philosopher

3. Jean-Paul Sartre and Morality: A Legacy Under Attack

4. Sartre Lives On

5. Forced Out of Vietnam: A Policy Analysis of the Fall of Saigon

6. Natural Law: Morality and Obedience

7. Cogito Ergo Philosophus

8. Le Racisme et le Socialisme: La Discrimination Raciale dans un Milieu Capitaliste

9. International Law: The Rise of Russia as a Global Threat

10. Citizen Obedience: The Nature of Legal Obligation

11. Jean-Jacques Rousseau: A Collection of Short Essays

12. Être Noir: Quel Malheur!

13. L'homme et le Racisme: Être Responsable de vos Actions et Omissions

14. Pennsylvania Inspired Leadership : A Roadmap for American Educators

15. Adult Education in America: A Policy Assessment of Adult Learning

16. Postcolonial Africa: Three Comparative Essays about the African State

17. Go Back Where You Came From

18. Retournez d'ou vous venez

19. Regrese de donde vino

TESKO PUBLISHING

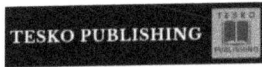

Other References: You may find other works by Dr. Ben Wood Johnson by visiting his blog.

MY EDUKA SOLUTIONS

BEN WOOD POST

www.benwoodpost.com

TESKO PUBLISHING
An independent publishing house

www.teskopublishing.com

BEN WOOD POST
www.benwoodpost.com

Striving to Survive: The Human Migration Story
BEN WOOD JOHNSON

www.ingramcontent.com/pod-product-compliance
Lightning Source LLC
Chambersburg PA
CBHW022112280326
41933CB00007B/353